Eat the Sky

Eat the Sky

poems and musings
by
h. duxbury

Eat the Sky
Copyright © h.duxbury

Photographs and cover design by h.duxbury.

All rights reserved. This book or any portion thereof may not be reproduced or used in any manner whatsoever without the express written permission of the publisher except for the use of brief quotations in a book review.

Published by h.duxbury.

First printing, February 2024.

h.duxbury
Ontario, Canada

www.hduxbury.com

ISBN: 978-1-7772131-3-8

For the ones who keep choosing love.

table of contents

Introduction 2
   eat the sky 4
Philautia 7
   an unlikely heart 9
   a thousand stories long 10
   dandelion heart 11
   spring planting 12
   softness still lives 14
   wildflower soul 16
   tangled 17
   softness rebellion 18
   unraveling 19
   the whole damn sky 20
   contradictions 21
   home 22
   stars and darkness 24
   twilight heart 25
   let me be a gentle wilderness 26
   warm tea 28
   a spell for self-acceptance 29
   breathing love 30
   dearest burden 31
   a beauty and a danger 32
   hope is a treasure 33
   anti-aging 34
   the fog 37
   my body 38

- the firefly 39
- morning body 40
- beauty & strength 41

Philia 43
- love your fear 45
- shortbread recipe 46
- autumn day 47
- custom fit 48
- the size of distance 49
- love letter from the cat 51
- if tenderness were an animal 52
- lessons in softness 53
- soft wishes 54
- yellow 55
- nest 56
- force of nature 57
- lighthouse 58
- love is not bondage 59
- instead of loneliness 60
- joy cartographer 61

Eros 63
- living tapestry 65
- forever 66
- all the end 67
- worthwhile 68
- wait 69
- the open door 70
- constellations 71
- atheism 72

burning	73
sunset	75
universe of two	76
stay	77
hydration	78
call and response	79
early mornings	80
wild mysteries	81
smile	82
the sky at the end	83
don't mourn	84
better	85
Agape	87
floating hope	89
wildflowers	90
drowning in beauty	91
streetlight omens	92
morning forge	93
warmth	94
always enough	95
little bird	96
choices	97
innocence	98
the price	99
after the storm	100
sunrise	101
smoke	102
the moths	103
a bird in flight	104

time 105
loving 106
lifelong lover 107
endings 108
in the morning 111
Acknowledgements 114
h. duxbury 117

Introduction

Eat the Sky is a love letter to love.

Oddly enough, most of the poems in this collection were written during one of the worst mental health periods of my life. A combination of crushing depression and completely unchecked burnout meant that I was barely functioning. Joy felt so far away it might as well have been in a different universe entirely.

And yet, in the midst of this, so much beauty.

Beauty that was found in the people and places I loved: friendships that were soft enough to hold all the rough parts, beloved pets who comforted and brought humour, forest paths filled with secrets and quiet.

The first time I truly felt joy again, the only word I could think of to describe it was "overwhelming". We forget how big it is, how much space it takes up.

This book is not about looking away from the darkness. It is about saving some space for joy. It is about celebrating love, connection, and hope in SPITE of darkness. We can hold both.

We CAN hold both.

From my heart and pen, thank you.

- h. duxbury

eat the sky

I describe the sky
in flavours:
peach and sugar and vanilla creams
cotton candy and lemon mousse.
Things soft
and sweet.

The sky does not judge.
Regardless of how your day went,
or what you might have said wrong
it moves and shifts,
and every moment is the only one
every day a different flavour of sky
every sky a story
and me, below
taking in as much of it as I can
as though my eyes are not enough
my heart so full of sky
I can almost taste it

the immensity
the fragility
of a moment

spreading inside my chest

maybe if I could swallow the sky,
my heart would finally be big enough to hold this world

Philautia

you are the beauty you see in the world

an unlikely heart

I was born
with an unlikely heart
neither fact nor fiction
neither broken nor whole
scattered like seeds,
carried on the wind
never missing, never found
I uncover it everywhere
constantly discovering, growing
into my
unlikely heart

a thousand stories long

You were my unbecoming

You found the dangling thread
in the comforting lie I was living
and tugged
kept tugging
until I was shivering in the harsh light and cold air

unlike you, though
I am a creator

spinning new warmth from old tales and heart strings:
a gown with a train a thousand stories long.

You could never create with me,
but were just what I needed
to start a new chapter

I am still learning how to wear my truth
not like armour
but like a breath

dandelion heart

I am a never settled mess
my head always seeking
something in the clouds
my feet always rooted in the ground
my heart trapped
somewhere between earth and sky
a dandelion gone to seed
trying to touch everything

spring planting

This spring I will plant myself in the earth--
fingers to the knuckle in damp soil
I will open myself to the sun again.

With dirt beneath my fingers
I will grow something beautiful.

softness still lives

Sometimes I fear
all the broken parts
have left me jagged
sharp to touch,
a danger to myself and others.
I fear that these honed edges
have punctured my tenderness,

but then
I find ways to wrap them
      in the gentlest shades of sunrise
      the velvet touch of my cat's fur
      the sweetness of a friend's laugh
and I know
the softness still lives.

wildflower soul

You can have a wildflower soul
but that does not make you
more
or less
beautiful
or powerful
or strong
than those in gardens.

We all have roots.
It always takes work to bloom.

tangled

Forgive me the tangled underbrush of my heart
but there is so much to see
under leaves
behind trunks
the rot under the log, life giving--
but maybe not for you.

Why do the poison berries always look the most sweet?
I promise the thorns won't kill you
if you move slowly, patiently
you can find secret places where beauty grows:
all soft petals
and sweetness like a summer berry

Forgive me the tangled underbrush
of my heart

so much grows
in its fertile soil.

softness rebellion

I am relearning
how to live with softness
in my body
in my heart

in a world that values hardness
leaning into my softness
is a radical act

unraveling

Some days it feels like the gentlest tug will unravel me like a worn sweater, heart strings and storylines collapsing on themselves in a tangled mess, just another thing to sort through, pick apart, make beautiful again.

the whole damn sky

I am neither sun nor moon,
on really magic days I am both --

I am the whole damn sky

contradictions

I am a creature of daylight:
greedy for sunlight
barefoot in the grass
I bloom like the flowers in spring.
Root down into warm earth
with fingers and toes.

I am filled with night:
dark shadows between my ribs,
burning in direct sunlight,
I shy into shadows.
Starlight shimmering under my tongue
I carry the eclipse in my eyes.

home

is not a place
it is a state of being
a feeling

like finally recognizing myself
again

stars and darkness

I have fought against my darkness
as I have fought against
the changing of the seasons:
full of terror
deep in my bones
for what the darkness means.

Finally,
I am learning to see the beauty
in the darkness
       the opportunity for stars
       for rest
to be gentle
with this most vulnerable
side of myself

twilight heart

My twilight heart,
shades of blue, and glimmering
with dew or frost or stardust.
It is a promise of magic
of real life

hovering between
grief
and ecstasy

Let's turn the lights off--
we won't need them soon.

let me be a gentle wilderness

Many will ask
for you to tame your heart,
to be docile.

I refuse.

I will keep my
wild, unruly feelings.

If I am to be a home
to wild things,
let me be a gentle wilderness
as much refuge
as risk.

warm tea

I hope
I learn more kindness
that my laugh lines become deep as canyons
visible from space
      a beacon in the darkness, declaring:
      "love lived here"
large enough to hold all the joy of a lifetime
deep enough to drown my sorrows

I hope
I still talk with my hands
wizened knuckles waving like tree branches
weaving stories,
spreading memories like seeds
I hope my lips are still too sensitive for hot beverages
that I still let my tea sit a little while before drinking
      a pause
      a breath
      to let something cool

a spell for self-acceptance

Take one part of the patience you give to the new clerk at the grocery store
Blend with a dash of the loyalty you give your lover, and a portion of the love you hold for others
Stir in the kind words you give your best friend on a bad day,
and warm it in the glow of pride you usually dampen down
Sprinkle generously with tenderness.

Stopper it carefully, so bad things cannot get in

Apply liberally, apply often.

breathing love

maybe I was born with my heart in my throat
maybe every breath has been a cycle of love coming
and going
maybe that is why I wear grief like a well-loved
garment
maybe that is why I choke on words and kindness
maybe that is why I so desperately hope to breathe
love into this world

dearest burden

Some days
my heart
my tender heart
is the heaviest
dearest
burden

a beauty and a danger

Be gentle with my jagged edges
and they will not cut you

Behold my raw self
glittering like ice
a beauty and a danger

I can break you, without meaning to
I can break myself as well,
hard edges cracking against one another

I hope someday I melt
I hope I flow like a river
like water
nothing but soft edges in my path
nothing but flowers in my wake

I hope I bring life by just existing

hope is a treasure

Hope is a treasure
I hide for myself

I find it in the soil
that I pat around growing roots
I discover it in the way the sunlight
slants through tree branches
and hiding in the soft fur
of my cat at midnight
I dig it out from between lines of text
in beautiful books
and spot it in the eyes of my most beloved people

I know I am a person who freezes

but I also know that hope, like the sun
will always find me
when it is time to bloom again

anti-aging

The advertisement glowing
on the tiny screen in my hand
promises
it can erase the lines from my face.

From between the images of shiny packaging
and glowing,
well made-up skin,
it whispers
that it can erase the life from my features.

It suggests
perhaps
that the crease between my eyebrows
      (inherited from my father
      and my love of summer sun)
is not as lovely
      as a smooth patch of skin

It suggests
that the lines beside my lips

    (mirrors of my mother's,
    a testament to stories told and laughter
    shared)
would be more beautiful
    if they didn't exist at all

It suggests
that the lines across my brow
are unlovely
despite the life and memories they connect

It suggests
if only I could erase these things that make me
singular

I could be more beautiful

if only I could look empty

I could be worthy

I block the ad.
Smile my crooked smile
(lips slightly turned down at the corners, a gap in my front teeth)

I let the creases and the crinkles say

I will not erase the marks of who I am
I will not regret the stories life has written on me

The ones who love me
can read our history in my face

the fog

the fog rolls in so softly
silently
it reminds me that i,
like the fog,
am temporary
soft
impossible to capture
impossible to tame

my body

My body I hold like a lover,
not because there are no flaws but because
it is precious regardless.

My body is the story I will write my whole life.

It is full of hard lessons and soft landings.
It is the first thing that taught me how to fall,

and where I learned how to stand back up.

the firefly

it was never you I was chasing
down those midnight paths

you were not the light in the dark
you were not the out of reach firefly

I was

morning body

In the morning
my body is a beauty
a marvel of soft hills, lush valleys,
a smooth flow of harmony,
like a song,
unstoppable as the tide;
before the world of sharp angles and rigid corners,
hard edges and deadlines,
she is a marvel of softness--

the heart that carries my soul

beauty & strength

give me flowers
and bright things with stingers

I love the beauty,
I love the strength to survive

Philia

friendship is the root of all love

love your fear

Tell me your fears, darling
let me hold them,
cradled in my hands

let me whisper words of hope,
stories of magic and love

until they soothe and settle.

Let me show you the bravery
of loving your fear tender.

shortbread recipe

you are now a mix of memories
the smell of baking
the sound of your laugh
melting
like shortbread on my tongue

your recipes
as much a mystery to me
as so much
of who you were

autumn day

To me you are an autumn day
born in spring, you hate the winter
and it's grasping cold

but you are warm

soft cozy flannel
and warm apple cider
on a rainy evening

you are a breath of fresh air
a sigh
a rest

custom fit

I never know where to put this love
it never fits in boxes
the only space designed to hold it
is your heart

the size of distance

missing you stretches like a band
across the space between us

fragments of measurement

kilo deca centi milli

that never capture the distance,
the empty pockets of time
that were supposed to be filled
with you

love letter from the cat

These are the days
I can smell sicky sweet sorrow on your skin,
like salt
and the struggle to breathe.

Do not be so fearful.

Be soft,
let your searching hands
find something to hold onto
in my fur.

Let me take your tears
and give you laughter
and warmth for when you are feeling cold
and lonely.

I can remind you of softness
when times are hard.

I am small
but I can help you carry this sorrow.

if tenderness were an animal

If tenderness were an animal, it would be a cat curled on your lap, all soft fur and quiet purrs. It is not that it does not have claws.

It is that it does not choose to use them.

lessons in softness

When I wake in the dark, I reach out, bury my fingers in your fur, feel the soft rumble of purr and the rise and fall of your breath, in time with my heart.

Your fur adorns everything I own.
What a blessing, to carry evidence of your love and affection everywhere I go.

A blessing, your lessons in softness

even in the darkest hours of night.

soft wishes

I wish for you
all fruit, no pit

but I know the hard part
is what lets beauty grow

yellow

I think of you
in honey yellow
dripping kindness
sticky with hope

soothing
to all the rough places
in my heart

nest

firm as a tree,
so rooted,
so reaching,
I bow when I must
and stand tall when I can.

I grow over the scars
and the lost moments,
keep them as stories in my bones.

Make a home in my arms,
a space soft and you-shaped,
for your most fragile dreams.

I cannot do everything,
but I will do everything to protect you.

I love to see you fly.
I love to see you return like the spring.

force of nature

When I wake, my stomach is a storm, a whirlpool, swirling and churning like the force of nature I am and we are and can be. Home has never been a stack of bricks so much as the swell of your laugh, the eternal technicolor of my heart, the stretch of your smile, so bright I believe it can vanquish all shadows. I cannot count the hands that have shaped me, but I can count the ones I quietly slipped pieces of my heart into and who held them gently, like a prayer. The only time I pray now is in the space between breaths when the beauty of a flower, or wave or small shiny beetle reminds me that miracles are everywhere. Never a word, but a swelling, a stretching. A storm, a tempest, the force of nature I am, we are, can be.

lighthouse

no matter the storm
you are still standing
to guide me home

love is not bondage

the love stories never discuss
how you can love so absolutely
without needing to win
to conquer
to own
How it is possible to just love
with no expectation

that love can be warm
and pure
without tying anything down

love is not a net
to catch others with

instead of loneliness

stretch across the bed
expansive as the night sky
pull the corners of the sheets out
a caterpillar cocooned
create a hurricane of coziness
a storm of which you are
the heart

you have always been holy
sacred as the dawn
stars in your eyes
and fire in your heart
you are what has been wondered at
and sought

your transformation
as brilliant as the sunrise

joy cartographer

It is not always easy finding your way in the dark
everything unfamiliar
taking new forms

but even the dark is not unlovely
clarity is often overrated and the dark
has stars
aurora borealis

Joy cartographer,
teach us how to find direction
even in the dark
do not be afraid to seek,
to map the unmappable

show us it is possible to navigate the impossible
the world needs those who can find the light
in the darkest times

and follow it

Eros

when intimacy meets lust

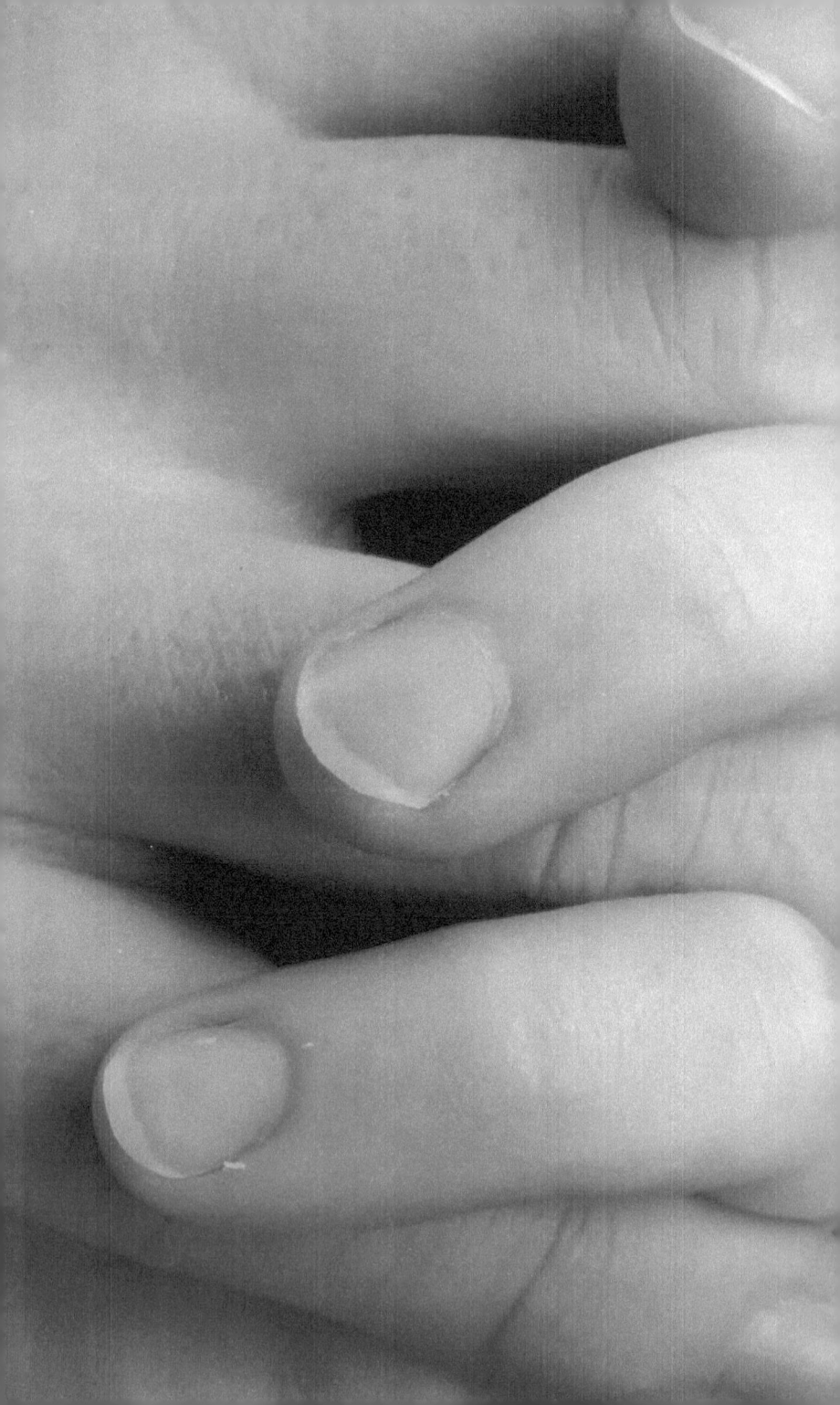

living tapestry

this skin
is a living tapestry
of scars and stories

I want you to read
to memorize every line
wrap up in one another
until our stories
blend together

forever

I no longer try to force
f o r e v e r
into someone's eyes

just take each day
as a step
in that direction

all the end

When you think of me
do you still see
the freedom of my heart
midnight swims under the stars
moonlight on water, music in our ears--
or is it nothing but darkness and fear?
A blank night sky, the broken parts?
Is it all the end, and never the start?

worthwhile

it has been nice
experiencing a love
that makes all the failed loves before
worthwhile

wait

do not give your heart away
just because they demand it

wait for the one who will tenderly
patiently
reach for your hand

who will be grateful
when you offer your heart
as well

the open door

You are not the open window
through which I feel the breeze

You are the open door
the chance of being free

constellations

I don't need to go outside
to see the stars
we can make constellations of our scars
we have all the galaxies we need
written in your face
with fingertips and lips
we write
our own maps of fate

atheism

you are an atheist, through and through
but I have always known
how to make you pray

burning

you
are all burning desire
and questions
with no answers

sunset

I always think of you at this time of year
of my green boots
of your smile at my open door
of the snow outside
and the heat within

of how the endings
all of them
managed to sometimes feel like beginnings

I knew where we were headed
and for once I didn't look away
from the horizon
like the sunset
I knew we had an ending

and that it would be as lovely
as you

universe of two

If I could build a ship
from hopes
and dreams
and long-distance phone calls,
I would fit it with sails made
from every message we ever sent
trying to translate our hearts
into a language that
that time
and our worlds
could understand

I would sail with you
away from minutes and latitudes

between the waves
and the stars
we could build a universe of two
and spend a lifetime
making stories with you

stay

the sky might be on fire
but we are both right here
with oceans of love between us
they can never make us disappear

hydration

there is nothing romantic
about drinking enough water

except for the hope
that it will earn me
more days with you

call and response

At night my hand rests in the center of your chest
your heartbeat gentle against my fingertips
my own heartbeat calling and responding,
blending until I cannot tell if it is your heart,
or mine,
or ours

early mornings

early morning
when you cannot tell night
from day
finds us wound together
so you cannot tell me
from you

wild mysteries

so
so aware

of the space your body occupied

the negative space

between yours
and mine

the wild emptiness

between my fingers

the dark mystery
of your mouth

smile

I am still in awe
after all the years
and all the words
of your ability
to strike me wordless
with a smile

the sky at the end

the night sky
never looked so beautiful
before you

some day
one of us will look at it
alone

how beautiful will it be?

don't mourn

I hope you never mourn me
but once in a tender moment
I hope you feel a bit of warmth
for what we almost had

better

love does not have to be forever
to change you for the better

Agape

love big enough to hold earth and sky

floating hope

Hope floats to me
a seed on the wind
lands softly in my cupped hands
light as air
glistening
with promise

a tender gift
from a delicate world

I open my hands
watch it float away

Hope
should never be caged

wildflowers

another word for wildflower
is weed

the stubborn ones
with deep roots
and tough stalks
that bloom ferociously
not beautifully

drowning in beauty

I am drowning in beauty
I can almost not breathe

over my head again

don't pull me up
don't wake me up

I am drowning in beauty
it is the only way I can breathe

streetlight omens

I wake in the dark
the window fogged by rain
the world outside
someone else's dream

On the drive to work,
the glow of the streetlights
reflects on rain-soaked pavement
like an omen
like a sign

what are you waiting for?
why don't you slow down?

morning forge

the sunrise is molten
a new day in the forge

and I don't need rose-coloured glasses
when the glow is painting everything pink

chasing the night across the sky

I turn my eyes toward the rising sun
hope that it can banish the night
from my eyes
too

warmth

it builds up in the corners of your eyes
like sleep on a lazy Sunday morning

rests between your fingers
toes cozy in wool socks
and in the steady rumble of a cat's comfortable
cuddles

I find it in your loud laugh
and in April sunshine

the casual smirk of an inside joke
and my favourite song

steaming in a beloved mug
and under blankets gifted and made

the gentle flicker of candle flame
and melting butter on fresh muffins

in my hands
in my heart

always enough

if it is love
it is always enough
love is a quality
not a quantity

little bird

a bird swoops past my feet as I walk
all wings and feathers
swift as a gasp

this little bird knows more of life
than I ever may

the distance between breaths
the weight of air
the flight of a moment

choices

the loss of innocence is inevitable
bitterness does not have to be

innocence

I sit still
and think of innocence.

The world moves around me
headlights shooting by like mortal time,
the streetlights turning hydro wires
to shimmering spider threads,
gossamer against a sky as dark
as the jumbled trash bags
huddled like lovers on the roadside.

The absence of stars goes unnoticed
for the twinkle of glass and metal
caught in the glare of passing headlights
that make shadows leap and dance
in the empty lot below me.

I think of innocence
as a cat bounds from a hedge
something tiny and unmoving
in its jaws.

the price

those who are capable
of great love
will always pay
in great grief

after the storm

the morning
smells like woodsmoke
and wonder

a promise of magic
hangs in the haze
of last night's storm

there is power in release
and there is power
in the rising

sunrise

Sunrise
has seen so many
of my most
    vulnerable
    wild
    raw
moments

as it rises,
so I, too, rise

smoke

on mornings like this
even the smoke from the local factory
can look beautiful--
soft, pastel peach and gold
drifting skyward
dreaming of clouds

the moths

in the morning when I wake
with last night's grief still crusted around my eyes,
the moths visit.

Pressed against the window edge,
the ceiling,
the door frame.

They are small,
dull,
easy to overlook.

Is this hope?

small,
dull,
easy to overlook.

a bird in flight

Love is a bird in flight,
something impossible to capture,
out of reach of our simple words
and simple boundaries.

There are no borders where love flies,
it is a danger and a beauty.

We hope it will roost beside us,
perch lightly in our hands,
but we can never hope to capture it
with nets
made of words.

time

I measure time in the colour of leaves,
the length of shadows in the evening
and the size of cloud my breath becomes
in the early morning.

I measure my life in hugs from friends,
letters in the mail
and the softness of my cat falling asleep against me.

If life is a journey, it is mapped
in the tracing of my hand on your arm,
joining constellations of freckles across your back.

I have had eras measured in jeans
that walk everywhere with me
until they are so soft they crumble.

If this is my life,
I hope that I never stop falling,
that I wear myself so soft
I eventually crumble.

loving

Love
is a state
not an intention

lifelong lover

in the kitchen, making dinner
in the garden, under the leaves
among the clover, tousled by bare feet
amidst the snowflakes landing on my nose

the words find me
they always come back

the dearest lover
of my life

endings

the sky is pink sherbert
lavender blush

were endings ever this sweet?

in the morning

I speak hope softly to the world
in the hope that it comes softly back
on moth wings,
gentle and unassuming

I know hope is not a beauty
but I write it every day
write to it every minute
odes to hope are written in my veins
and bone marrow

Hope is the ghost that roams the halls
when I am empty
whispering
that the morning always smells the most beautiful
and we should meet there

Acknowledgements

An acknowledgement section for a second book would be impossible without a long line of people who supported me before, during and after the first. Many of the poems I write are inspired by others & inspired by the world around me. I am so grateful for every person who has inspired and supported me and my creations over the years.

However, a few people were specifically instrumental in helping this book move from idea to reality.

Emilia – From the moment we met, you have taught me about the bravery and beauty in vulnerability. Thank you for everything you did for this book – from helping to choose fonts to reading drafts, this little spot of joy would not have been what it is without you.

Jessie – there is too much to thank you for, spread over so many years. You know so many of my secrets and shadows and have shared so many of yours that I hardly can imagine who I would be without you somewhere in my life. Thank you for still being here. And for being the one person who has now proofread both of my books.

Ari – thank you for stepping forward to be one of the first people to read this collection, for giving your opinion and thoughts and for sharing your art and creativity with the world in all the ways you do! Ari and their work can be found at @ari.para.art on Instagram.

Dan – Many of the poems in this book would never have been written without you. Thank you for being a safe place, an inspiration, and for seeing the beauty in me at my worst. Most importantly, for showing me what love can be.

h. duxbury

h. duxbury, lives in Ontario, Canada, where she was born and raised. Other than writing, she enjoys a variety of creative outlets, getting outside, and spoiling her cat.

h. duxbury is also the author of *phases*, her debut collection of poetry, and Capture the Beauty: A Creative Companion. You can find more of her work on social media @hduxburypoetry, or on her website www.hduxbury.com

A note on type:

The typeface used for body text and poem titles is Cardo, designed by David Perry, and used under the SIL Open Font License v1.10.

The typeface used for chapter titles is Isabella Script Monoline, designed by Seniors Studio, and used under the Desktop EULA 2.0 from Creative Market Labs Inc.

The typeface used for the book title is Isabella Script Regular, designed by Seniors Studio, and used under the Desktop EULA 2.0 from Creative Market Labs Inc.

www.ingramcontent.com/pod-product-compliance
Lightning Source LLC
Chambersburg PA
CBHW031121080526
44587CB00011B/1065